THE HIGH-TICKET SALES POCKET GUIDE

A 12-STEP SCRIPT TO SELL MILLIONS WITH YOUR CELLPHONE

CRAIG JOHNSON

Contents

ABOUT THIS POCKET GUIDE

This is your "Pocket Guide" to selling high-ticket products or services. A pocket guide is a concise book you can read in under 30 minutes that addresses a specific problem you're facing. It's compact enough to fit in your pocket for easy reference whenever needed.

The 12-Phase Sales Script presented in this guide is called the Million Dollar Script. It has earned this name because it consistently generates significant revenue for those who use it.

Apply this Million Dollar Script when engaging prospects via phone, in person, or even through text messages.

This is the same script I've used to generate over 7-figures from my advice, services, online courses, coaching, and high-ticket seminars.

Initially, I only taught this script within a $10,000 program I launched years ago. Witnessing how quickly it helped people improve their sales, often within a single day, I was inspired to write this book.

I've seen this script transform business owners' trajectories almost instantly, sometimes on the very first day they learn it. After observing such dramatic shifts time and again, I felt compelled to share this knowledge more widely.

Once you've gone through this pocket guide, you'll know exactly what to say during a sales conversation.

However, you might be grappling with other challenges not covered in this guide, such as crafting a compelling offer, refining your messaging, mastering marketing, producing sales videos, and building a brand.

If you need help with those areas, I recommend exploring Upstride Growth at Upstride.us.

WHO THIS BOOK IS FOR

This book is tailored specifically entrepreneurs and business owners looking to start or boost sales of their premium products and services, including:

- Coaching or Consulting

- Digital Marketing

- Done-for-You Services

- Online Courses

- Masterminds

- Professional Services

- Agency Services

- Events and Seminars

- High-End Software

In essence, if you're selling or aspiring to sell high-end products and services, this book will help you increase your sales and train your sales team, if applicable.

For salespeople aiming to boost their commissions, this book provides invaluable strategies. Moreover, it equips you with a versatile skill set that will serve you well as a commissioned salesperson today and as a potential entrepreneur in the future.

The techniques shared in this book will not only enhance your professional life but will also enrich every aspect of your personal journey.

HOW I LEARNED TO SELL

Before becoming an 7-figure earner, an Amazon best-selling author, and a real estate investor, I was bartending as a college dropout.

Growing up in a small California town and oldest child, my home life was tumultuous. I lost my father at a very young age and my mother was mostly absent. I was forced to grow up rather quickly an learn how to take care of myself. Holidays and birthdays were never the same and my world was turned upside down.

I struggled to maintain my school attendance. My lack of social skills made me a target for bullies, and I had few friends. This isolation, however, allowed me to devote considerable time to reading and computer programming.

I became passionate about reading and computers, and acquired knowledge I believed could benefit others. Unfortunately, no one took me seriously or listened to me, preventing me from sharing these valuable insights.

Have you ever felt you had something important to share that could help people, but no one would listen? It's an awful feeling. This experience is why I always make time for people at conferences, taking photos and chatting. I understand the pain of being ignored and don't want others to feel that way.

Eventually, I convinced myself to go to college and study medicine. While this solved my immediate visions of my future, it did not solve my immediate money problems. It also did not match my history of skills. However, it did help my social skills which are crucial for sales. I then dropped out of college, and as one does, gets their real estate license. I got a job selling timeshare, learned a new skill, and then became a top salesperson for Wyndham Resorts.

The skill that made this possible was Neuro-linguistic programming (NLP) sales. I learned this technique and learned to sell my own advice and experience—the very thing people had dismissed throughout my life.

Through determination and a willingness to learn, I mastered the art of rapport and the sales pitch. This skill not only helped me succeed in direct sales but also enabled me to initially build a six-figure business selling my own consulting, coaching, and educational products.

I now dedicate myself to teaching others this transformative skill. My mission is to help those who, like my younger self, have something valuable to offer but lack the tools to make themselves heard. Through my teachings, I've helped create thousands of successful businesses by sharing the power of effective communication and sales techniques.

This book contains a part of that knowledge—a simple sales script to help you sell your products and services at premium prices. Keep it handy and share it with your team. It's my hope that this guide will serve you well in your sales endeavors.

The Million Dollar Script

The Million Dollar Script outlines 12 phases of a sale:

I. Rapport

II. Expectations

III. Decision Makers

IV. The Reason

V. Dig

VI. Tried

VII. Current and Desired Situation

VIII. Why

IX. Admission

X. Commitment

XI. Customized Close

XII. Price

The 12 phases serve as a framework to gather essential information from prospects, enabling you to craft a tailored pitch that resonates with their needs. Adapt your approach based on the prospect's responses, skipping phases if you've already obtained the necessary information. Remember, this is a flexible guide, not a strict script.

#1 GOLDEN RULE

If a prospect is ready to buy, facilitate the purchase immediately. Don't force them through the entire process if they've already decided.

PRO TIP:

When prospects answer your questions, listen more and speak less. Avoid unnecessary chit-chat (except during the rapport-building phase), tangents, or storytelling (unless addressing an objection). Let the prospect do 95% of the talking. Your goal is to gather information, not to dominate the conversation.

PHASE 1: RAPPORT

In the first few minutes of the call, focus on building rapport through friendly conversation. Ask about their location and how their week is going. Find common ground to establish a connection.

To facilitate this, consider researching their social media profiles beforehand to identify shared interests or topics you can discuss.

Begin with a question like, "Where are you calling from today?" Then, follow up with relatable comments such as:

• I remember visiting there ...

• My Dad is actually from there ...

• Oh, isn't it pretty warm/cold there this time of year ...

People prefer buying from those they can relate to, and finding common ground is key. Encourage them to talk about themselves, as this helps build rapport and provides valuable insights.

Use these techniques to encourage self-disclosure:

Mirroring: Repeat the last few words they say with an upward inflection to prompt elaboration.

For example:

Prospect: "We relocated here two years ago for our children's education."

You: "Oh, for your children's education?"

Prospect: "Yes, we weren't satisfied with Chicago's school system."

You: "You weren't satisfied with Chicago's school system?"

Prospect: "Right, we felt it was too liberal and didn't want our children indoctrinated."

Use this information to find common ground:

You: "I understand completely. I'd consider homeschooling before putting my child through that."

Prospect: "Exactly! The current situation is concerning!"

Matching: Align your energy level with theirs, even if it may not be "your cup of tea". If they're reserved, maintain a calm demeanor. If they're enthusiastic, match their excitement. People are more likely to buy from those who resonate with their communication style.

Phase 2: Expectations

This phase is where you set expectations. You outline the format of the call and get the prospect to agree to it. When a prospect agrees to a specific conversation structure, it becomes much easier to maintain control and keep the discussion on track.

Here's my preferred approach:

You: "Are you ready to get started, [FIRST NAME]?"

Them: "Sure."

You: "Great. Here's how these calls typically go... [Frame this as a standard procedure rather than giving instructions.] It's similar to a doctor's appointment. I'll ask you some questions about your business [or health, investments, mindset, etc.] and your challenges. Then, I'll diagnose the problem and suggest a solution, much like a doctor would recommend a treatment or prescription. If we have a solution that can address your problem, and we're confident we can help, I'll provide more information about our offerings. You can then decide if you'd like to proceed. Does that sound okay?"

Them: "Yes, that sounds good."

By structuring the call this way, you've taken control of the conversation. You've not only outlined the process but also secured their agreement to follow it. This makes it easier to keep the discussion focused and productive.

Without this framework, the conversation lacks direction and can become chaotic. Remember, sales thrive on clarity, not confusion.

Once you've established this agreement, you can move on to the next phase of the call.

Phase 3: Decision Makers

Understanding who's needed on the call to seal the deal is vital. Ideally, you want all decision-makers present.

If you're only speaking with one, there's a high chance they won't effectively relay the information to the others. They might also falter when faced with questions or objections. So, while it might not always be feasible to have every decision-maker on the call, striving for it can make a world of difference.

Many salespeople use the direct approach: "Do you need to get your spouse on the call to make a decision?" However, I've found a subtler way, allowing the question to blend seamlessly into the conversation.

A common question we ask is, "What do you do?"

With that as a segue, after discussing their job, you can pivot to their personal life: "I'm curious, are you handling things solo, or do you have a family?"

If they're solo, you're good to proceed. If they mention a family, based on the rapport you've built, casually inquire, "What does your spouse do?" After they respond, gently probe, "Are they on board with you pursuing [DESIRED OUTCOME], like shedding some pounds or growing your business?"

Most times, they'll confirm the spouse's support. From there, perhaps transition to discussing their kids. After all, most people love talking about their children. It ensures the conversation feels genuine and devoid of sales pressure.

For B2B interactions, adjust your approach slightly: "I meant to ask earlier, are you the sole captain of this ship, or do you co-pilot with a business partner?"

If they're solo, you can move forward. If they mention a partner, delve deeper: "When considering doing business with another company, how do you and your partner approach decision-making?"

This way, you can gauge if the partner's involvement is pivotal and decide how persistent you should be in getting them on a call. But tread carefully. Being overly aggressive can jeopardize the deal. Remember, there's no harm in scheduling a follow-up call if needed.

THE SILENT KILLER TIP - FROM CRAIG:

If both partners are on the call, you can often identify which one is The Silent Killer. The talker is the one that does the most talking and interacts with you the most frequently. Many times this is the husband and the wife stays somewhat quiet, or vice versa. If it's a business partner, there will usually be one that is more forward and one that is more silent.

The one that is more silent is the one you must watch out for. We call this The Silent Killer. They're the ones who will keep quiet until it's time to deny the sale. You want to make sure they feel heard and respected. Get them to chime in, and get them to ask questions or offer objections so that you can overcome them.

You do not want to wait until the end of the call when they spent the last hour hearing you give all the attention to their partner. Now you make the pitch, and you basically have to start all over with them. Not good.

PHASE 4: THE REASON

In this section of the sales call, your goal is to have the prospect verbally state the reason for the call. Even if it seems obvious, they need to articulate it to bring it to the forefront of their mind. This helps them focus on why they initiated this conversation and the pain points surrounding that reason. People are more likely to make a purchase when they feel the cost of enduring the pain outweighs the cost of resolving it. By having them discuss their pain openly, we encourage them to truly feel it.

Begin by asking why they scheduled the call and what specific assistance they need from you. AN effective way to phrase this is:

> "So, the first thing I always like to ask is, why
> did you book a call with me today? What do
> you need my help with specifically?"

This question has two parts, and some prospects may address both in their response. If they don't, it's crucial to follow up.

An ideal response might be:

> "Well, I saw that you [accomplished notable
> thing] and found that impressive. I really
> need help with [problem] because [reason
> it's urgent now]."

However, you'll rarely receive such a complete answer. Often, they'll address only one aspect, such as:

> "Well, I really need help with [problem]."

This is good because they've vocalized their need, but they haven't explained why they chose you specifically.In this case, you can follow up with:

"Got it. So you reached out because you need help with [problem], but why did you choose us out of all the options available?"

This prompts them to validate your credibility, which is more powerful than you stating it yourself.

Once you've established their need and your credibility, ask the most crucial question:

"But why now? Why is it so important to solve this right now?"

This question reveals the underlying pain or urgency driving their decision. Understanding this is key to tailoring your approach and solution to their specific situation.

Remember, you're not just selling a product or service; you're offering a solution to a problem that's affecting their life or business in a significant way. By uncovering and addressing the real pain points, you can position your offering as the path to resolving their most pressing issues.

Phase 5: Dig

This phase can be skipped if they thoroughly explored why they need help in Phase 4, but typically, it's necessary to delve deeper into their pain points.

It's crucial for them to truly feel the impact of leaving their problem unsolved. We need to obtain specific, detailed answers. If they provide a general response, simply ask, "Can you expand on that? Tell me more about it."

Additional ways to uncover the pain include:

- Why do you think this problem exists?

- What have you tried to fix it?

- How long has this been a problem?

- Is this problem affecting your life in other ways, and how?

For instance, when someone mentioned not wanting to handle their own sales calls or manage their sales team, the underlying reason was their desire to spend more time with their newborn.

Us: "Oh, is it a boy or girl? What's the name? Charlie? That's adorable. You know, many parents hire nannies or night nurses, but it seems you really value connecting with your child. What makes that so important to you?"

Them: "Well, my father wasn't around much when I was growing up, so I don't want to repeat that with my own child."

Us: "Your father wasn't present much during your childhood?" [Mirroring]

Them: "Yeah, honestly, it affected both me and my sister in many ways."

Us: "How so?" [Remember to furrow your brow to show concern when asking sensitive questions.]

Them: "We lacked a male role model. No one taught us how to ride a bike, or in my case, how to fix things around the house. My mother always had to hire handymen."

Us: "It sounds like you're determined not to let Charlie have that same experience?"

PRO RAPPORT TIP:

Use phrases like "sounds like" when a prospect shares something. This helps you connect, shows you're listening, and validates their experience. It also encourages them to continue talking without resistance.

Them: "Absolutely. I've promised myself I'd never let that happen to him. That's why being there for him is so important to me."

Us: "I understand. We hope we can help make that a reality for you.Would you mind if I asked a few more questions to ensure we can achieve that?"

Remember, we're not selling sales management. We're selling what sales management can provide – in this case, the opportunity to be the father he always wanted. We started with "I need help with sales" and uncovered a powerful, personal story about his relationship with his father.

When the prospect is focused on their deeper motivations rather than your offer, it becomes significantly easier to sell your solution.

The key is to evoke emotion while simultaneously showing genuine care. This is a skill that requires teaching, development, and nurturing.

This process isn't easy, especially when selling your own offer. I typically spend 4-7 weeks training a closer, with ongoing nurturing throughout their tenure.

The effort is worthwhile. A well-trained sales team can generate substantial revenue while freeing up your time. In my experience, investing in developing this skill in your team is invaluable.

PRO TIP:

Avoid asking "Why?" when a prospect expresses their feelings or beliefs. Instead, use "What" or "How" questions:

- What makes you say that?

- How did you come to that conclusion?

- What do you think is the reason for that?

- How do you think that happened?

PHASE 6: TRIED

Midway through the call, it's crucial to understand what the prospect has already attempted. At this point, their emotions should be heightened, making them more likely to share detailed information.

"What have you tried so far to address this issue?" This question not only highlights their frustration in attempting to solve the problem independently but also provides essential information for tailoring our pitch.

Understanding their previous efforts allows us to differentiate our product effectively. We typically offer either a unique solution or a more efficient approach to methods they've already explored.

This knowledge is vital to avoid suggesting something they've already tried, which could be detrimental to the sale. Such a misstep might lead the prospect to believe we're not listening or lack the expertise to help them.

Armed with this information, we can present our solution in a way that acknowledges their past attempts while highlighting our unique value. For example, when selling a coaching program for speakers seeking more bookings:

Instead of simply stating, "We show you how to cold call event organizers," we could say:

"We provide a proven cold calling script that 99% of speakers don't know exists. I understand you've tried cold calling before, but our clients are consistently amazed at how quickly they secure bookings using this unique approach."

This strategy preemptively addresses potential objections and demonstrates the value of our offering. However, this tailored approach is only possible when we take the time to understand the prospect's previous efforts.

Phase 7: Current and Desired Situation

Now we need to understand their current position and desired destination. The first question in Phase 7 focuses on identifying their exact location in the journey to solving their problem and what that entails. This is their Current Situation.

Unless you've already obtained this information, ask about their current status using the most quantifiable metrics relevant to their situation. For example, if they're trying to increase income, inquire about their current earnings. For weight loss goals, ask about their present weight. If they aim to become a public speaker, ask how many engagements they're currently booking per month.

For instance, in a weight loss scenario, you might ask, "To better understand our starting point, would you be comfortable sharing your current weight?"

PRO TIP: To ease the request for sensitive information, phrase it as "Would you be comfortable with" instead of "Are you opposed to". This approach is more positive and inviting.

Depending on what they've shared about their reasons for the call and previous attempts, you can ask follow-up questions such as:

- What are your goals with XYZ and how far short of that goal are you falling?

- What have you tried so far to XYZ?

- How long have you been dealing with this problem?

- What does your current process to achieve XYZ look like?

- How many hours a week are you spending on XYZ?

- How happy are you with the way you are currently doing XYZ?

Next, we determine their Desired Situation – where they want to be.

To set proper expectations, ask, "If you were to work with us or join our program, where would you want to be in 12 months to feel the investment was worthwhile?"

PRO TIP: Framing the question this way encourages clients to set realistic expectations, allowing you to exceed them.

Be cautious about discussing your best results or making specific claims immediately. Instead, let the client set the bar, then aim to surpass it.

If a client still presents unrealistic expectations, use the Down to Earth Close to reset them:

"I understand you want [unrealistic expectation], and that's an admirable goal. To ensure we set realistic expectations, if we were to [achieve a more realistic outcome], would you be satisfied with that result?"

Once you've established their current situation and desired outcome, you can move on to exploring their underlying motivation – their WHY.

PHASE 8: WHY

This is the phase where we understand WHY they want the Desired Situation. Why do they want the result that they want? Is it just about making more money? Or is there a deeper motivation, like buying a house because their spouse has been asking for years? Often, you'll find that people don't really want more money; they want to avoid disappointing their loved ones or prevent their spouse from leaving them.

We revisit Phase 4, delving deeper into the reasons behind their desire to solve the problem. By associating it with a specific result, we earn the right to bring it up again without seeming redundant.

We might say something like:

- OK great, so you'll be happy if you lost 50 pounds?

- OK great, you'd be happy if you made an extra million dollars?

- OK great, you'd be happy if your dog was a 7 out of 10 on the obedience scale?

Now ask them why they want the result they want. But don't ask, "Why?" Instead, ask, "What is driving you to want XYZ" or "How would your life be different if you had XYZ?" Remember to use WHAT or HOW in lieu of WHY whenever possible.

- May I ask what is driving you to achieve that goal? In other words, if you made an extra million dollars, how would that affect you or change your life? What would that look like?

- May I ask what is driving you to lose 50 pounds? In other words, if you lost 50 pounds how would that change your life? What would that look like?

PRO TIP: The best way to get someone to share specifics about their motivations is to simply ask, "What would that look like?" This non-aggressive approach helps you gather necessary information without seeming intrusive.

At this point, they'll begin sharing their reasons. Use mirroring and "sounds like" statements to encourage them to elaborate, as you did in Phase 5.

If you encounter resistance, try this approach:

> "The reason I'm asking about how your life would change with an extra million dollars is that our founder loves featuring customer success stories. He's passionate about sharing his customers' wins. People don't just want to hear that someone made money; they want to know how it changed their life. It's more impactful to share that you were able to buy a bigger house for your growing family or pay for a loved one's medical treatment."

FUN FACT: The reason WHY someone wants something always boils down to either LOVE or STATUS. Whether it's losing weight, making more money, or achieving any other goal, the underlying motivation is typically tied to one of these two factors.

Understanding whether we're dealing with love or status, and what that looks like for our customers, is crucial in this phase of the process.

PHASE 9: ADMISSION

Now comes the most crucial phase of the call: the Admission. Our goal is to have the prospect acknowledge their need for assistance.

CRITICAL: It's essential to get them to verbally admit that they're unsure of how to proceed or that they urgently require help. If they don't recognize their need for assistance, or if they fail to articulate it, closing a sale becomes impossible.

Ask this key question: "What's preventing you from accomplishing this independently, without any external support?"

This crucial insight comes from marketing expert Sam Ovens. When you ask the key question, you're looking for one of three responses. If you've navigated the conversation correctly up to this point, your prospect should provide an answer along these lines:

- I don't know how to do it.

- I want to follow a proven process from someone who's already done it.

- I want to get there faster.

If you've navigated the conversation correctly up to this point, your prospect should provide an answer along these lines. It's crucial not to proceed until you receive a response that aligns with at least one of these three admissions.

PHASE 10: COMMITMENT

After the customer has admitted they need help, we must secure their commitment to solving the problem immediately.

A effective approach is to ask, "When do you want to fix this?" If they say "now," follow up with:

- "How committed are you to making that happen?"

- "Will you do the work and take action?"

- "Are you coachable?"

- "Will you provide the information we need to get started?"

Tailor these questions to your specific offer. This shifts the focus from the sale to the customer's responsibility. Once they commit, proceed to the next phase.

If they suggest a later start date, probe further:

- What makes you say a month?

- Any reason you don't want to fix it right now?

- You booked a call for today, so what is making you want to wait?

Often, they'll realize the urgency. If not, try the Procrastination Close:

"Have you been postponing solving this problem? How has that worked out? The truth is, it's never the perfect time to start. Life keeps happening.If you truly want to solve this, shouldn't you commit even when conditions aren't ideal?"

Another effective technique is the Take Away Close, which plays on the "we want what we can't have" psychology:

"We only work with committed clients who are ready to go. If you're not fully committed, you likely won't see results. We're not here to convince you – just to determine if you're a good fit.Would you like to end the call, or discuss how we can solve your problem?"

This approach often works well and ensures you're not selling to uncommitted clients who may struggle to achieve results.

Once you secure commitment, move on to Phase 11.

SIDE NOTE: Resistance from prospects is called objections. Handling objections is a crucial skill in sales. While a perfect sales script can convert without objections, most salespeople will encounter them. We offer extensive training on objection handling in Upstride Growth.

PHASE 11: CUSTOMIZED CLOSE

This is the core of the entire script. If you've executed everything correctly up to this point, you're about to deliver a pitch to the customer that will feel as if the entire offer, product, or service was specifically designed for them.

You'll want to describe the customer's identity as they described themselves. Describe what they want in their own words. And describe the most relevant portion of your program or product that can help them achieve their goal.

It should feel so personalized that it's as if, on the day they were born, the doctor said, "We're going to create a product specifically for this baby."

Now you say something like, "Alright, I believe I have enough information now, and honestly, I believe we can help you. Would you like me to share how?"

PRO TIP:

Always say "I believe" instead of "I think". "Think" implies uncertainty, while "Believe" conveys confidence. People trust believers.

✓ – I believe we can help you. Would you like me to share how?

X – I think we can help you. Would you like me to share how?

They will most likely say YES, and then you use the following Customized Close framework to make your pitch:

> "Well, our area of expertise is helping [CUSTOMER IDENTITY] to get [RESULT THEY WANT] so they can [BYPRODUCT OF RESULT]. And we do that by [OFFER]. Now, this may not be for you, but I'll let you decide. Does that sound like a good fit so far?"

PRO TIP:

When you say, "This may not be for you," it puts the customer in a frame of mind where they want to justify why it is for them. Humans always want what they can't have. So it makes them commit even more to your offer - especially after the offer you have explained is obviously perfect for them.

This customer will almost always say yes because it has to be a fit. All we did was literally repeat back to them exactly who they are, what their problem is, and what they will get as a result of solving the problem.

Using an example from my business at Upstride.us, let's say someone was on a call with us about getting help with creating a winning offer. In this scenario, we encounter two distinct types of individuals: one who has never crafted an offer, and another who has tried and failed. The solution we're providing can assist both; there's no need to design two separate offers. Instead, we slightly adjust the positioning of our single offer based on the client's feedback about their current situation and aspirations.

While the following positioning adjustments may seem minor, they can have a profound impact on the outcome. Our objective is to make the offer feel tailor-made for the individual.

The first individual is a single dad who has never created an offer before. He mentions he is struggling with deciding on what to sell, how to package it, and how to articulate it to his audience. Furthermore, he's uncertain about identifying his target audience. Given that he's running a single-parent household, he also has limited time to make these decisions.

Someone from my team might say something like:

"Our area of expertise is helping solopreneurs, especially those with limited time and support, quickly figure out their first offer, how to position that offer, and how to package and deliver it so you don't pull your hair out with fulfillment. Our goal is to get them their first clients ASAP, without spending weeks or months on complicated marketing. We can expedite the process because we've worked with thousands of entrepreneurs to create profitable offers. We know what works and what doesn't, saving our clients a significant amount of time. Does that sound like a good fit so far?"

Now let's look at the second individual. This guy has already created several offers, but they haven't been successful, then we might respond:

> "Our specialty lies in assisting solopreneurs who've previously launched offers that didn't meet expectations. We help them swiftly craft an offer that sells and position it properly using a framework that has proven successful hundreds of times with our existing clients. Many of these clients had multiple unsuccessful offers before seeing results with us."

Regardless of their situation, both should respond with a "YES." Why? Because we've tailored the positioning of our offer to feel custom-made for each individual.

The difference is very slight, but the way in which your offer is articulated can be worlds apart. It's your articulation that will make the sale, not your offer. The only way to properly articulate it is to ask questions and plug the answers into that articulation.

Once they confirm that it's a good fit, you immediately say, "Great! Can I share how it works?" At this point, you're going to assume the sale and walk them through what it will be like when they sign on with your company. You're not going to ask them for money or if they have their credit card ready - none of that old-school nonsense. You are going to assume they have already bought, and you are doing nothing more than walking them through the onboarding process.

This is called the "How It Works" Pitch. Creating your own "How It Works" Pitch is essential, and while I can't guide you on crafting it in detail here, I can provide an example. The key is to clearly describe what happens from the time they sign up until they begin seeing results. Present this process step-by-step, framing each step as a benefit. Remember, this will be unique and tailored to your product and business.

Here's an example of a "How It Works" Pitch we've used:

> "So, your next call will be with your Offer Creation Coach, Amanda. She will conduct an onboarding interview, posing a series of specific questions. This helps us un-

derstand your goals and familiarize ourselves with past strategies you've attempted. We'll make sure to schedule that call with Amanda before we end our current conversation. After that, you'll receive an email containing login details. This lets you dive straight into the training area and view the timetable for upcoming sessions. Once you've gone through the training materials, you'll complete your "Offer Ideation Sheet" based on Craig's guidance. You'll then discuss this sheet with Amanda on your subsequent call. She'll work with you to ensure your offer is structured in a logical and compelling manner - designed to be easily marketable, without causing you undue stress during delivery. This way, you can attract as many clients as you desire without being overwhelmed by the fulfillment process. You'll work with her twice a week for a span of 12 weeks. This ensures you receive ample support to quickly acquire your first several clients. Our goal is to simplify the process for you and make this easy. In addition, you'll receive a ticket to an in-person event with Craig. There, he'll delve into the entire system and also introduce advanced topics to aid in your scaling efforts."

Once you finish your "How It Works" Pitch, the next thing you should ask is simply "Do you have any questions?" At this point, they will likely ask multiple questions about your offer to gain clarity on how it works, what the results could be, etc. You'll go ahead and answer those questions, and if you hear an objection, you will handle it.

Do not volunteer any more information than what they ask. If you start talking about all the features of your program, you can kill the sale with information overload and talk about things they don't want. Stick to what they ask. Eventually, you'll get to the magic question...

NOTE: If you are a solopreneur and do not have a sale team. You will of course not offer the second call. You will then say something like:

> "So, I'd like to welcome you aboard and Customize your Offer. I have a few specific questions to help me understand your goals and familiarize myself with past strategies you've attempted. After that, you'll receive

an email containing login details. This lets you dive straight into the training area and view the timetable for upcoming sessions. Once you've gone through the training materials, you'll complete your "Offer Ideation Sheet" based on my guidance. You'll then discuss this sheet with me on a subsequent call. I'll work with you to ensure your offer is structured in a logical and compelling manner - designed to be easily marketable, without causing you undue stress during delivery. This way, you can attract as many clients as you desire without being overwhelmed by the fulfillment process. You'll work with me twice a week for a span of 12 weeks. This ensures you receive ample support to quickly acquire your first several clients. My goal is to simplify the process for you and make this easy. In addition, you'll receive a ticket to an in-person event with me. There, we'll delve into the entire system and also introduce advanced topics to aid in your scaling efforts."

Customize this script to your own busienss and how you'd like to proceed with onboarding and training.

PHASE 12: PRICE

In this final phase, we confront the most significant challenge: price.

It's crucial to never mention price until the client asks. Continue answering questions until they inquire about the cost. If they don't ask after several rounds of questions, simply keep saying, "Do you have any other questions about getting started?"

When they inevitably ask for the price, it's vital that you didn't volunteer it earlier. This helps you maintain control of the conversation. If they already know the price, it becomes easier. You can simply ask, "When would you like to schedule your onboarding call? Great. What kind of card will you be using today?"

You'd be surprised how many people will readily provide their card information. However, if they're unaware of the price, state it simply: "The investment is $5,000."

After announcing the price, it's critical to REMAIN SILENT!! Do not speak until they do, even if it takes 1-2 minutes. This silence is crucial; breaking it prematurely could cost you the sale.

I once had a prospect who talked to themselves for over 100 seconds, going from "I can't afford this" to "I can't afford NOT to do this" without any input from me.Their next words were, "Do you take Mastercard?"

At this point, you'll either secure a sale, receive a deposit, need to schedule a follow-up call, set up a payment plan, or address objections.

THE OBJECTION PHASE

In a perfect world, if this sales script is executed flawlessly, you will get no objections. Any objections you do receive will merely be requests for reassurance. However, we don't live in a perfect world, and not everyone will execute this script flawlessly every time. Even if they do, it's always possible the prospect will have concerns that need to be addressed.

When that happens, it's time to overcome objections. While handling objections is not within the scope of this booklet, I'll provide a few quick ways to handle some common objections. If you need more help, consider exploring Upstride Growth.

OBJECTION: "I've tried products like this before and they haven't worked. What makes yours any different?"

Most salespeople would respond by talking about how great their product is, its features, success stories, and why it's the best. This is the worst approach. If you've done this previously, it indicates a need to improve your sales skills. Pay close attention to the content in this book.

When a prospect asks this, they're not really asking about your product. What they say and what they're thinking are often different. They're likely recalling a specific negative experience with a similar product and want to avoid repeating it.

Address this by saying: "I understand you've had experiences with similar products that didn't work out. To best answer your question, could you share a specific example of what happened with a prior product you purchased?"

They will describe a situation, and if they're not specific enough, encourage them to provide more details.

Once you understand their specific concern, you can address it directly. For example, if they mention lack of support in a previous program, and your program offers more support, you can highlight this difference.

OBJECTION: "I'm on vacation for the next month and can't take advantage of the program until then, so I'll wait till I get back."

This objection is easy to overcome, especially for coaching programs. Acknowledge their concern and offer a solution: "I understand you don't want to lose a month of service. If you enroll today, I'll add an extra month to your coaching contract. You can go on vacation and return with the full time you paid for. Plus, if you decide to access the members area before you return, consider that bonus time.Does that work for you?"

OBJECTION: "I want to talk to a client about their results first."

This objection is about trust. Either you lack public client testimonials, and therefor should get some posted, or the prospect doesn't fully trust the ones you've shared. Address this with transparency: "I understand you want to speak with our clients, but we prefer not to turn them into salespeople. Here's what I'll do: If you enroll today, I'll put in writing that once you access the program, you can network with existing clients, including those who've provided testimonials. If you find any testimonial we've posted is inaccurate, I'll refund your money and let you keep the program. Are you comfortable with that?"

Remember, these techniques work best when you have a quality product and genuine testimonials. Always prioritize ethical sales practices and delivering value to your clients.

BONUS: The Possession Close

Here's a powerful closing technique to use when a prospect is still on the fence. You can say:

"I understand you're hesitant about making this investment. Let me offer you a 24-hour trial to fully experience the product before you buy. You'll be able to log in, watch the modules, network with other members, and even ask them if they found their investment worthwhile. We'll schedule a follow-up call in 24 hours. At that time, you can decide whether to keep the program or not. If you choose to keep it, we'll process your payment. If not, we'll revoke access and part as friends. How does that sound?"

This technique is called The Possession Close. I first learned about it when I was bartending. My co-worker, an experienced bartender, taught it to me when I was struggling increase my sales. Instead of asking customers if they wanted a shot before handing it to them, he told me to hand the shot to the customer first, then ask if they wanted it. Once customers had physical possession of the shot, they were much more likely to say yes.

Years later, I applied this same principle to my online course business, resulting in an additional $1 million in enrollments annually.

NOTE: If you're concerned about prospects downloading all your content and leaving, this is unlikely to happen within a 24-hour window. However, if you're still worried, you can limit access to a portion of the product – just make sure it's compelling enough to showcase your value.

BONUS: The 1 to 10 Close

Finally, this is my favorite close. I'll give you an example from a recent call I had with a prospect.

Them: Craig, I'm just really nervous that your certified closers won't be able to close as well as the ones I already have.

Me: I totally understand. Let me ask you a question. On a scale of 1 to 10, how good do you think you are at teaching someone to sell?

Them: Probably two or three. I don't really have much sales training experience.

Me: Got it. So with everything you know about me and my company and what we've done in the industry, on a scale of 1 to 10, how good do you think I am at teaching people to sell?

Them: Well, probably a 9 or 10.

Me: Got it. Well, let's say I am an 8, to be conservative. Forgetting the current situation we're talking about, if you were a betting man and you had to put money on whether or not an 8 would outperform a 2 at teaching someone to sell, or for that matter anything, who would you bet on?

Them: Yeah, I get your point. I would totally bet on you.

Me: And you already know that if we make just one extra sale per month, we completely cover our fee AND take the massive burden of managing your sales team off your shoulders. You yourself said that you would bet on us, so the only question is...Are you knowingly going to make less money? Or are you going to do what you already know you need to do and let us work together to blow up your sales?

They wired the money 10 minutes later.

Most of the time prospects already deep down know what the right answer is, but they have to work through it. They have to say it out loud. If they don't say it out loud, they can't make a decision. Once they hear themselves say what makes sense, now they can do what makes sense.

The 1 to 10 Close works best when you have authority in the space and a logical path to the conclusion that they will get the result much easier or faster if they had your help rather than doing it on their own.

AN IMPORTANT NOTE ABOUT MARKETING

Marketing is the foundation that makes sales both possible and more effective. Excelling in marketing strategies such as lead generation, social media content creation, copywriting, and email nurturing significantly eases the process of closing prospects during sales calls.

When generating leads, it's crucial to establish credibility, clarity, and authority through your marketing efforts. Without these elements, sales calls can become extremely challenging. While it's still possible to close a sale using effective scripts, in today's digital age where prospects can instantly research you online, it's vital to have a strong online presence and compelling content to showcase. If you'd like to learn more about techniques and programs I teach, do a search for Upstride Digital Marketing or check out my youtube channel at YouTube.com/@upstride.digital.marketing.

To enhance your marketing and sales skills, I offer online courses and coaching at Upstride.us and I encourage you to take full advantage of these resources to boost your marketing and sales expertise!

WHAT'S NEXT ...

I sincerely hope you have enjoyed this guide. It took time and effort to ensure I clearly articulated the sales script I've used to completely change my life and the lives of thousands of my clients.

In fact, this Million Dollar Script is responsible for creating multiple 6- and 7-figure businesses from scratch—businesses that came to me with literally zero sales to start. I've tried my very best to give you the proven script for High Ticket Selling in this short pocket guide.

I am 100% certain this guide will skyrocket your sales once you have someone on the phone. But mastering the art of the sale is just one piece of the puzzle. Ask yourself:

- How do I craft an irresistible offer that resonates?

- With so many potential products or services, which one should I choose?

- Once I've pinpointed that ideal offer, how can I articulate its value compellingly?

- How do I fill my calendar with sales appointments?

- Building a recognizable brand isn't instant; where do I start?

- How can I systematically attract and nurture leads, ensuring a steady flow of potential clients?

We both understand that how you handle a sales call isn't the sole challenge in your journey. There are several problems to solve if you want to become a millionaire. After all, isn't that the essence of a millionaire? Someone who relentlessly tackles obstacles, and is rewarded generously for their efforts and perseverance.

At this point, you have two options:

Option 1: Use this guide to fix the part where you don't know what to say on the phone, and figure out all the other problems yourself.

Option 2: Join Upstride Growth and get help with the entire picture. As well as join thousands of others inside this premium community designed to support you in growing a business that gives you ultimate freedom. Our goal is to make it as easy as possible for you to do so.

Remember, the biggest expense in your business is money you could have made but didn't. If you're tired of leaving money on the table, consider joining the UG family by going to Upstride.us.

About the Author

Craig Johnson is a seasoned digital marketing expert, Amazon bestselling author, and dynamic speaker known for his impact on the U.S. entrepreneurial landscape. As the CEO and founder of Upstride Growth®, Craig has dedicated his career to helping entrepreneurs and business owners scale their online presence. Originally from Thousand Oaks, CA, and now based in San Diego, Craig's journey began at 17 when he launched his first business—a limousine service—while still in high school. This early venture sparked a passion that led him to leave college and dive full-time into entrepreneurship.

With an eclectic background spanning studio work in Hollywood, health and computer science education, bartending and fine dining, Craig ultimately found his true calling in digital marketing, where he's thrived for over 20 years. Over his career, he has helped to built multiple million-dollar ventures, including United Real Estate Media, and helped generate over $20 million in revenue across several businesses—a success he attributes largely to the Million Dollar Script detailed in his book. As a master on stage, Craig has achieved over $1 million in sales in a single day using strategies he now shares on YouTube. His mission is to empower others with proven, high-impact strategies for financial freedom and business success.

NEXT STEPS

One afternoon, after a brisk jog in the park, I returned home and spotted an odd sight on the kitchen table: a tall, clear glass bottle filled with green juice.

To give some context, I'm a big fan of green juice. Not the sugary stuff, but the organic kind made from spinach, kale, and all those other leafy superfoods. I drink it daily, sometimes twice, and it easily costs me over $200 each month.

Curious about this unexpected bottle, I asked my fiancé about it. Without saying a word, my fiancé pointed to the fridge and threw the door open. Inside sat my usual store-bought green juice.

"See this?" raising an eyebrow.

"Green juice?" I replied, a little confused.

"Yes," was the reply, "But take a look at what's inside. Preservatives, added sugars... and it's six dollars a bottle!"

My fiancé then pointed to the mystery bottle on the table and asked, "And what about this one? Can you guess?"

"Uh... green juice?" I ventured.

"Exactly! But I made this myself with our new juicer." holding up a compact black device. "It cost us less than $50. With just some fresh veggies and water, it produces triple the juice you get in a store-bought bottle—and it's pure, with none of the junk."

I did a quick calculation in my head: this fresh, homemade green juice cost pennies compared to the store-bought version. I'd been needlessly spending over $200 a month on something I could have easily made at home, minus the fillers I didn't need.

In that moment, I realized this expense was rooted in a simple lack of knowledge. I hadn't known how easy it was to make green juice at home. And this, I realized, is a common experience. So much of what costs us—whether in time, money, or effort—comes from things we simply don't know yet.

Think about your own business. My green juice oversight cost me $200 each month. What's the cost of not knowing how to get more clients or grow your brand efficiently?

If that resonates, that's why I built Upstride Growth. My mission is to make the process of building a successful business easier, smarter, and more accessible for anyone ready to take control of their own success.

Upstride Growth and the Legacy Builder Program is a thriving community of thousands of driven individuals, all uniting under shared aspirations and goals. If you're interested in becoming part of the family, visit Upstride.us.

Regardless of your choice, I appreciate the time you spent reading my book. It means the world to me.

www.ingramcontent.com/pod-product-compliance
Lightning Source LLC
Chambersburg PA
CBHW061258140726
47998CB00006B/2269